Fact Finders™

Questions and Answers: Countries

Iran

A Question and Answer Book

by Brandy Bauer

Consultant:
Hossein Akhavi-Pour, PhD
Professor of International Economics
Hamline University
St. Paul, Minnesota

Capstone
press

Mankato, Minnesota

Fact Finders is published by Capstone Press,
151 Good Counsel Drive, P.O. Box 669, Mankato, Minnesota 56002.
www.capstonepress.com

Library of Congress Cataloging-in-Publication Data
Bauer, Brandy.
    Iran: a question and answer book/ by Brandy Bauer.
    p. cm.—(Fact finders. Questions and answers. Countries)
    Includes bibliographical references and index.
    ISBN 0-7368-3752-3 (hardcover)
    1. Iran—Juvenile literature. I. Title. II. Series.
DS254.75.B38 2005
955—dc22   2004009810

Summary: Describes the geography, history, economy, and culture of Iran in a
    question-and-answer format.

Editorial Credits
Donald Lemke, editor; Kia Adams, set designer; Kate Opseth, book designer; Nancy Steers,
    map illustrator; Wanda Winch, photo researcher; Scott Thoms, photo editor

Photo Credits
Art Directors/C. Rennie, 9; Art Directors/John Ellard, 14–15; Art Directors/M. Good
12–13, 20; Art Directors/Tibor Bognar, cover (background), 1, 4, 25; Corbis/Bettmann, 7;
Corbis/Paul Almasy, 23; Corbis/Reuters/Issei Kato, 19; Cory Langley, cover (foreground),
11, 21; Peter Arnold Inc./Still Pictures, 17; Photo courtesy of Alberto Lopez, 29 (coins);
Photo courtesy of Morris Lawing, 29 (bill); StockHaus Ltd., 29 (flag); SuperStock/Robert
Llewellyn, 27

Artistic Effects
Corel, 24; Photodisc/Siede Preis, 16

1 2 3 4 5 6 10 09 08 07 06 05

Table of Contents

Features

Where is Iran?

Iran is located in the Middle East. It is slightly larger than the U.S. state of Alaska.

Iran borders three bodies of water. The Caspian Sea lies to the north. The Persian Gulf and the Gulf of Oman are south of Iran.

The Elburz Mountains stand along Iran's northern border. ▶

4

Map of Iran

Legend

✪	Capital
•	City
|||||	Desert
▲	Mountain
⛰	Mountain Range

TURKEY
ARMENIA
AZERBAIJAN
Caspian Sea
TURKMENISTAN

•Tabriz
Elburz Mountains
Mount Damavand
Mashhad•

✪Tehran
•Qom Great Salt Desert

Zagros Mountains
AFGHANISTAN

IRAN

IRAQ

KUWAIT
•Shiraz
Zahedan•

PAKISTAN

Persian Gulf

SAUDI ARABIA
UNITED ARAB EMIRATES
Gulf of Oman

OMAN

Scale
0   175   350 Miles
0   175   350 Kilometers

Deserts and mountains are Iran's main landforms. The Great Salt Desert covers part of central Iran. The Elburz Mountains stretch along the northern border. The Zagros Mountains are in the west. Mount Damavand is the country's tallest peak.

When did Iran become a country?

Iran has been a country for thousands of years. It was once called Persia. A series of kings, or shahs, ruled the land. In 1935, Persia became known as Iran.

In 1941, Shah Mohammad Reza Pahlavi took control of Iran. By 1979, many Iranians were unhappy with the shah. They thought he had too much power. Iranians wanted more rights, such as freedom of speech. They forced the shah to leave during a **revolution**.

Fact!

Iran means "Land of the Aryans." The Aryan people were some of the first settlers in the area.

In February 1979, Ayatollah Ruhollah Khomeini greeted followers in the capital city of Tehran.

Ayatollah Ruhollah Khomeini became the new ruler of Iran. He was an Islamic religious leader. Khomeini and his followers wrote a new **constitution**. It made the Islam religion the law of Iran.

What type of government does Iran have?

Iran's government is a **theocratic republic**. Religious leaders rule the country. A group of religious men choose Iran's **supreme** leader, called the *faqih* (fah-KEE). The *faqih* serves for life. The *faqih* makes sure the government and the people follow the laws of Islam.

Iranians elect a president to head the **executive branch**. In Iran, the president can choose any number of vice presidents. The president also chooses cabinet members to help run the government.

Fact!

Iran has the lowest voting age of any country. All people 15 years of age and older can vote in elections.

A painting of Khomeini covers the wall of an Iranian building. Khomeini was Iran's supreme leader from 1979 to 1989.

The main part of Iran's **legislative branch** is the Majlis. The 290 members of the Majlis approve cabinet members and help pass laws. A Council of Guardians makes sure each law follows the Islamic religion.

What kind of housing does Iran have?

Most Iranians live in cities. Some people own or rent modern apartments. Others live in houses made of mud or brick. Iranian homes are often small. Some of the richest people live in larger houses with gardens.

Where do people in Iran live?

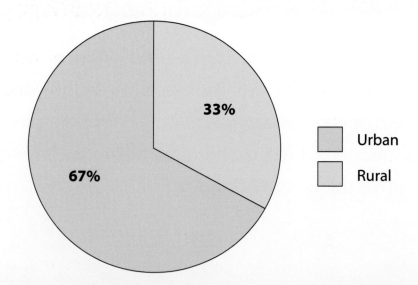

33%

67%

Urban

Rural

Many people in Iran live in mud or brick houses.

Outside cities, many Iranians live in mud houses with one or two rooms. Families often use carpets or cushions instead of furniture.

Iran also has small groups of **nomads**. These people live in goat-hair tents. They carry their tents from place to place.

What are Iran's forms of transportation?

In Iran, taxis, cars, and buses are the main ways people travel. In cities, traffic is a big problem. Cars cause air pollution. Heavy traffic also leads to many accidents.

Iranians also travel on trains and ships. The country has about 4,500 miles (7,000 kilometers) of railways. Ports sit along the Persian Gulf. Ships come to ports carrying oil and other goods for trade.

Fact!

In Iran, men and women cannot sit by each other on city buses. But they can ride in taxis together.

Streets are often crowded in Mashhad and other large cities.

Iran has more than 300 airports. The country's main airport is in the capital city of Tehran. Planes fly from Tehran to other Iranian cities. They also take people to countries around the world.

What are Iran's major industries?

Mining is important to Iran's **economy**. The country has a large supply of natural gas and oil. Much of the oil comes from the Persian Gulf. Iranians also mine iron ore, copper, and coal.

Agriculture is another important **industry** in Iran. Farmers grow wheat, rice, fruits, and nuts. They also harvest spices, such as saffron. Some farmers raise animals for meat, leather, and wool. Weavers use wool to make carpets.

What does Iran import and export?	
Imports	*Exports*
food	carpets
industrial services	fruits and nuts
military supplies	petroleum

The National Iranian Oil company drills for oil in Iran. Oil is the country's most important natural resource.

Fishers in Iran catch tuna, shrimp, and lobster. They also catch sturgeon in the Caspian Sea. Sturgeon eggs are used to make a salty dish called caviar. Iranians ship caviar to countries around the world.

What is school like in Iran?

Iranian children must go to school until age 11. They begin five years of primary school when they are 6 years old. They can then spend three years in middle school.

Students study many subjects including math, science, and religion. Iranian children study Persian, also known as Farsi. It is Iran's official language. Students also learn Arabic and another language, such as English or French.

Fact!

The Iranian school week lasts six days. Students must go to school every day except Friday.

In Iran, girls go to different primary schools than boys.

Many students attend high school for three to four years. After high school, students can take a test to go to college. Iran has many large colleges and universities.

What are Iran's favorite sports and games?

Soccer is a popular sport in Iran. Iranians play soccer in clubs or on city streets. They also enjoy watching the national soccer team.

People in Iran enjoy many other sports. Wrestling, basketball, volleyball, and table tennis are popular. On weekends, many Iranians go to the mountains to hike or ski.

Fact!

Ancient Iranians invented polo, a ball game played on horseback.

An Iranian soccer player (left) goes for the ball at the 2004 Asian Cup.

Iranians also play games. Chess started in Iran hundreds of years ago. Today, people play chess in parks, teahouses, and at home. Iranians also play backgammon and cards.

What are the traditional art forms in Iran?

Iran is famous for beautiful carpets. Weavers make carpets in many colors and sizes. Some carpets sell for thousands of dollars. In 2000, Iranian weavers finished the world's largest carpet. It is longer than two basketball courts.

Some Iranian artists paint small pictures and designs. ▶

Iranian weavers make carpets with colorful patterns.

Other traditional arts include painting and **calligraphy**. Many artists paint small scenes called miniatures. With calligraphy, people write words in a fancy style. Calligraphy often appears on the sides of Iranian buildings.

What major holidays do people in Iran celebrate?

Nowruz is the biggest holiday in Iran. It is the Iranian New Year. Nowruz takes place on the first day of spring. The celebration lasts 13 days. Shops, banks, and offices are closed during the holiday. People visit friends and family. On the last day, Iranians have picnics with music and games.

What other holidays do people in Iran celebrate?

Birthday of the Prophet Mohammad
Islamic Republic Day
Mother's Day
Victory of the Islamic Revolution

On the 13th day of Nowruz, Iranians set their tables with traditional items.

Iranians also celebrate Islamic holy days. During the month of Ramadan, Iranians don't eat or drink between sunrise and sunset. At the end of the month, they celebrate with a feast called Eid al-Fitr.

What are the traditional foods of Iran?

Iranians eat common foods, such as grains and vegetables. People eat bread at almost every meal. They buy fresh bread from local bakeries. Iranians eat rice and vegetables for lunch and dinner.

Most meals also include meat. People in Iran do not eat pork because of their religion. Instead, lamb is a common dish.

Fact!

Iranians make rose water from flower petals. They use rose water as a perfume and to season food.

People in Iran often meet with friends at teahouses.

Iranians often drink tea. Most towns and cities have teahouses. People meet at teahouses to drink, eat snacks, and talk with friends.

Another favorite drink is *doogh*. It is made with yogurt, mint, and water.

What is family life like in Iran?

Families are the center of Iranian life. Many Iranians have large families. Children, parents, and grandparents often share one home. The father is usually the head of the family. Women often cook meals and clean the house. Today, women living in cities also work outside the home.

What are the ethnic backgrounds of people in Iran?

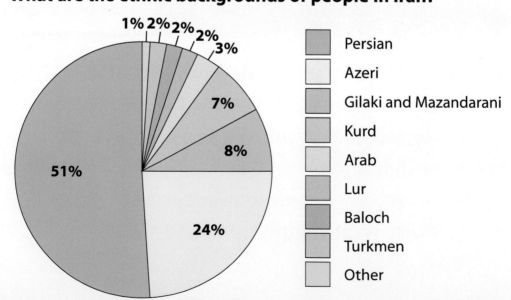

Legend:
- Persian
- Azeri
- Gilaki and Mazandarani
- Kurd
- Arab
- Lur
- Baloch
- Turkmen
- Other

Pie chart values: 51%, 24%, 8%, 7%, 3%, 2%, 2%, 2%, 1%

Iranian families often eat meals together.

Most Iranian couples have many children. Since 1975, the country's population has doubled. More than half of these people are under 30 years old. Today, many young adults work to make Iran a better place. They are helping shape the country's future.

Iran Fast Facts

Official name:

Islamic Republic of Iran

Population:

69,018,924 people

Land area:

631,663 square miles
(1,636,000 square kilometers)

Capital city:

Tehran

Average annual precipitation (Tehran):

10 inches (25 centimeters)

Languages:

Persian (Farsi), Arabic, Kurdish, Balochi, Turkish

Average January temperature (Tehran):

38 degrees Fahrenheit
(3 degrees Celsius)

Natural resources:

copper, natural gas, petroleum

Average July temperature (Tehran):

95 degrees Fahrenheit
(35 degrees Celsius)

Religions:

Islamic*   98%
*89% of Iranians practice a form of Islam called Shi'a; 9% practice Sunni Islam.
Other   2%

Money and Flag

Money:

Iran's money is the rial. In 2004, 1 U.S. dollar equaled 8,776 rials. One Canadian dollar equaled 6,967 rials.

Flag:

Iran's flag has green, white, and red stripes. The words "Allaho Akbar" are written 11 times on both the green and red stripes. In the Arabic language, these words mean "God is Great." The symbol of the Islamic Republic of Iran is in the center of the flag.

Learn to Speak Persian (Farsi)

Most people in Iran speak Persian, also known as Farsi. Learn to speak some Persian words using the chart below.

English	Persian (Farsi)	Pronunciation
hello	salaam	(sah-LAHM)
good-bye	khodahafez	(koh-dah-ha-FAYZ)
please	lotfan	(LOHT-fahn)
thank you	mercee	(MER-see)
yes	baleh	(BAH-lay)
no	na	(NAH)
welcome	khoshamadid	(KOH-shah-mah-deed)

Glossary

calligraphy (kuh-LIG-ruh-fee)—the art of drawing or painting words

constitution (kon-stuh-TOO-shuhn)—the system of laws in a country that state the rights of the people and the powers of the government

economy (e-KON-uh-mee)—the way a country runs its business, trade, and spending

executive branch (eg-ZEK-yoo-tiv BRANCH)—the part of government that makes sure laws are followed

industry (IN-duh-stree)—a single branch of business or trade

legislative branch (LEJ-iss-lay-tiv BRANCH)—the part of government that passes bills that become laws

nomad (NOH-mad)—a person who travels from place to place to find food and water

revolution (rev-uh-LOO-shun)—an uprising by the people of a country that attempts to change its system of government

supreme (suh-PREEM)—the greatest, best, or most powerful

theocratic republic (thee-oh-KRAT-ik ri-PUHB-lik)—a government ruled by religious leaders; the president and officials of a theocratic republic are elected by the people.

Internet Sites

FactHound offers a safe, fun way to find Internet sites related to this book. All of the sites on FactHound have been researched by our staff.

Here's how:
1. Visit *www.facthound.com*
2. Type in this special code **0736837523** for age-appropriate sites. Or enter a search word related to this book for a more general search.
3. Click on the **Fetch It** button.

FactHound will fetch the best sites for you!

Read More

Doak, Robin S. *Iran.* First Reports. Minneapolis: Compass Point Books, 2004.

Greenblatt, Miriam. *Iran.* Enchantment of the World. New York: Children's Press, 2003.

Teece, Geoff. *Islam.* Religion in Focus. Mankato, Minn.: Smart Apple Media, 2004.

Walsh, Kieran. *Iran.* Countries in the News. Vero Beach, Fla.: Rourke, 2004.

Index